NEW FOREST DRIFT

A Photographic Portrait of Life in the National Park

SALLY FEAR

For Claire Thompson
with Best wishes

Sally Fear

First published in 2006
by Perspective Photo Press
7 Nepean Street
London SW15 5DW

10 8 6 4 2 1 3 5 7 9

Produced by Julian Calder
Designed by Louise Millar

ISBN 0 9553253 0 7

Printed by EBS, Italy

Front cover: New Forest ponies coming down the driftway on the Slufters drift at Broomy, 2003
Back cover: Head Agister, Jonathan Gerrelli, surveys the ponies heading for the pound at Blackfield and Hilltop, 2005

To the Commoners of the New Forest

"It is an arduous job going out to see
what has happened to your animals.
The commoners do it for love."

"The New Forest
is an area of
international importance.
It is Britain's richest
'Nature Reserve'."

COLIN TUBBS

Contents

Foreword
by Oliver Crosthwaite Eyre
The Offical Verderer

The New Forest is more than just a beautiful and unique landscape, it is an environment shaped by the activities of its inhabitants over a thousand years. The exercising of ancient local rights to depasture animals has created the heaths and woodlands that make up the Forest that we know today.

Sally Fear's photographs are a powerful representation of the fact that, behind the beauty of the Forest, there lies a living and breathing tradition of commoning that has been practised by local families for many generations.

Viewed together, these pictures can help teach us the meaning and importance of sustaining and supporting commoning, without which the Forest would wither and change. This book shows, in a simple and moving way, that it is the love of the Forest still held by these families, father and son, mother and daughter, that allows commoning to continue to exist.

With the creation of a National Park, the Forest has now entered yet another landmark stage in its long history. Sally Fear's superb photography reminds us of the important fact that the Forest landscape is man-made and is the product of a rich local cultural heritage. This book is a celebration of those traditions and recognition of their invaluable contribution towards the ongoing conservation of England's newest National Park.

Introduction

by Sally Fear

When I came to the Forest and experienced my first New Forest pony drift I encountered an unchanging landscape, a sense of history and a well established community of commoners.

I was concerned that their work was not appreciated. In 2005 the New Forest was designated England's eighth National Park and the commoners were anxious about the changes that National Park status would bring.

I have always loved ponies and am naturally drawn to those who work with animals, so I began to record the commoning way of life. The New Forest has been photographed numerous times but no one has documented its working community. Photography is about communication and the best way for the public to appreciate the work of the New Forest commoners is if they can see it for themselves.

Our home has commoners' rights and we run three ponies on the Forest. This has taught me a great deal and I realise how fortunate we are that the commoners manage the Forest on our behalf and for the enjoyment of the millions of tourists who visit the Forest every year. Without them, there would be no New Forest and no National Park.

My photographs are a testimony to the work of the commoners. I hope that the New Forest National Park Authority and the New Forest commoners will work together in order that the New Forest we treasure can be conserved for future generations.

Commoners of the New Forest

The New Forest is a region of 90,000 acres (approximately the size of the Isle of Wight) with its own laws and customs, lying between the Southampton water and the River Avon, in Hampshire.

The Forest has existed for centuries, originally as a hunting ground and a source of timber for shipbuilding. The Forest is made up of heathland, lawns for grazing animals, enclosures and marshy bottoms, which together create a unique habitat for a wide range of widelife. Commoners, the people who farm and live on the Forest and who hold commoning rights over it, have a unique way of life that has not changed for hundreds of years. One theory is that the rights predate the Forest and were simply codified and regulated over the centuries.

These ancient 'rights of common' have led to a form of farming called commoning. The browsing and grazing of the commoners' animals has created a landscape that is rich in rare and unusual wildlife habitats and has led to the animals being called the 'architects of the forest'. The exercise of common rights is probably the only efficient and cost-effective way of managing such a large area of lowland heath. Just as the common rights are of ancient origin, so many of the methods of livestock management have remainded largely unaltered over the centuries.

People born into commoning are proud of their long family histories. They are fiercely protective of the traditions in which they were brought up and are determined to see them survive. Until very recently, the practising commoners were almost exclusively members of the old Forest agricultural families. Today some residents who have moved into the area have become interested in the value of the custom and have begun to run a few animals on the Forest. Although they are welcome, they lack the knowledge and skills that underpin the unique complex agricultural system and often regard their animals as pets.

Today there are approximately 500 practising commoners who are responsible for the 7,000 animals (mainly ponies) on the Forest. Exercising common rights is no longer profitable and the old commoning families run stock on the Forest because it is a tradition and because they love the way of life. 10% of the families own 80% of the stock and if they were to drift from commoning, there would not be many animals left on the Forest.

The commoners' interests are protected by the Verderers' Court, a body made up of five elected and five appointed officials. They look after the commoners' rights and work to preserve the natural beauty and traditional character of the Forest. The Verderers employ Agisters to look after the animals on the Forest.

Despite their crucial contribution to the maintenance of the Forest, commoners often feel misunderstood and undervalued. They are harrassed by the increasing demands of those who use the Forest for recreation and their animals are often killed or injured by traffic in the Forest. The Commoners' Defence Association and the elected Verderers protect their interests but perhaps the greatest threat to this ancient way of life is the chronic shortage of affordable housing.

The dramatic increase in property prices – small-holdings often start at twice the price of an average house which has put ownership of land beyond the average commoner. Land that has belonged to commoning families for centuries is rapidly being lost. As a result, many young people now have to choose between living with their parents in order to continue with the way of life, or moving out of the area.

19

"10% of the commoning
families own 80% of the stock,
so if these families ever drift
from commoning, there
won't be many animals
left on the Forest."

The Pony Drifts

New Forest ponies run wild on the Forest but they are all owned by commoners. Once a year it is essential that all the stock is rounded up for health checks, for marking and to wean the foals that have been born on the Forest. This is the time when surplus stock is removed from the Forest and taken to the sales. The round-ups, organised by the Agisters, are called pony drifts. There are usually about 40 drifts during late summer and early auturmn.

For each drift, the Agister formulates a plan with his commoners, deciding from which direction to approach the ponies. The riders distribute themselves accordingly and the walkers (commoners on foot) are positioned in likely escape routes. The riders must have an intimate knowledge of the Forest as the drifts move at great speed and taking a wrong turning or having to negotiate a bog during a drift could destroy a day's work. The expertise of the riders and the agility of their horses justly commands great respect.

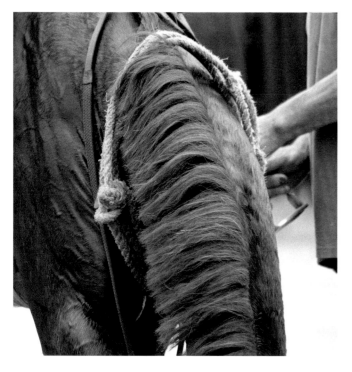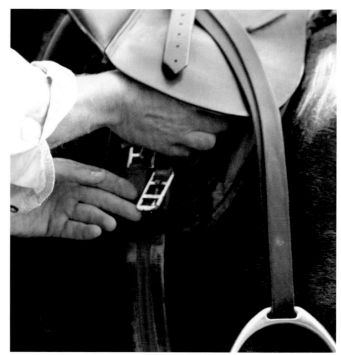

The drift is a magnificent sight with up to a hundred ponies at a time moving across the Forest at full gallop. The pace at which the ponies are driven is breath-taking and the ride can be hazardous even though the riders are as skilled in the saddle as any cowboy.

New Forest ponies move at great speed and have extraordinary stamina. They can go like the wind. At the start of the drift, some will take off at a fast gallop and can cover a couple of miles before giving in and being guided into the pound. Others will slow down after half a mile or so and allow themselves to be gently trotted in.

The wild ponies have the advantage over the riders. They can cross a bog at great speed, but the pursuing pony with a rider on board may find it impassable or the pony – and rider – can end up in the bog.

New Forest ponies are sure-footed riding ponies. They know exactly what they are doing and can turn very quickly. If a commoner is mounted on one when drifting, he or she can 'go out the side door' very easily if they don't hang on tight.

In the Pound

On a good day, a drift will bring in around 100 ponies. Once the Agister in charge of the drift has brought in all the ponies he can, he informs the mounted commoners and the walkers. They check that everybody who started out with them has returned and if someone is missing, the Agister sends out a search party.

The ponies are firmly secured in the pound. There is much excitement discussing the drama of the morning but there is still work to be done and the fire is prepared immediately for the branding irons.

As soon as they have taken care of the needs of their saddle horses, the commoners move to the pound to look for their ponies. There may be some surprises: a mare that hasn't been seen for several years may suddenly show up with a beautiful filly foal on her; a favourite mare may be lost and another may come in lame or injured. The ponies are wild and the public are warned to stand clear. The commoners know what they are doing and move expertly between the animals to avoid flying hooves. In order to examine all the stock, they isolate a small number of ponies at a time and drive them into a smaller pound called a crush. The aim is to keep the mares with their foals, but inevitably some get separated and there is often agitated calling from one to the other.

Once in the crush, the Agister moves deftly and quickly amongst the ponies, skilfully cutting or 'marking' their tails, stuffing the hair in his back pocket as he goes. Every pony that comes in on the drift has its tail cut to indicate that the owners have paid the marking fee. Each Agister has his own version of the tail mark and every commoner living in a particular Agister's area will have that Agister's tail mark put into all his animals.

The ponies are inspected by their owners and, if any are in poor condition, they are loaded onto a trailer to be taken back and cared for on the owner's holding. The ponies the owners want to sell at Beaulieu Road are also loaded up. Those foals staying on the Forest are branded, wormed and sometimes given a fluorescent collar to give the animal some protection against night-time traffic.

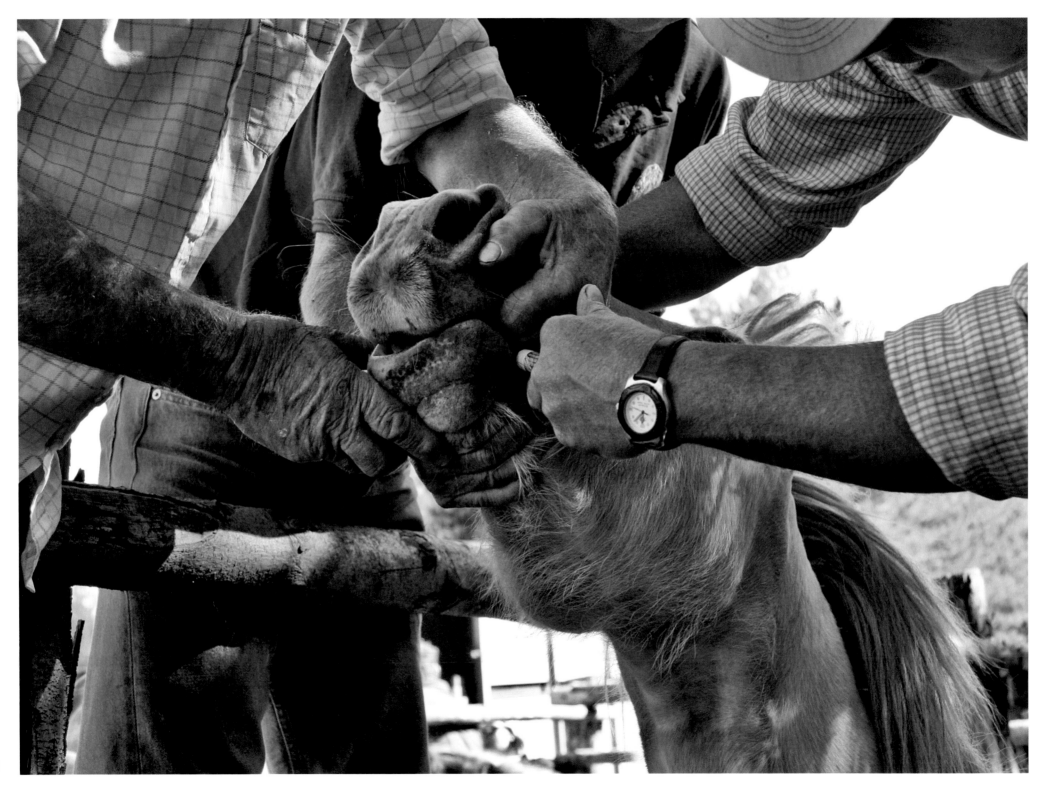

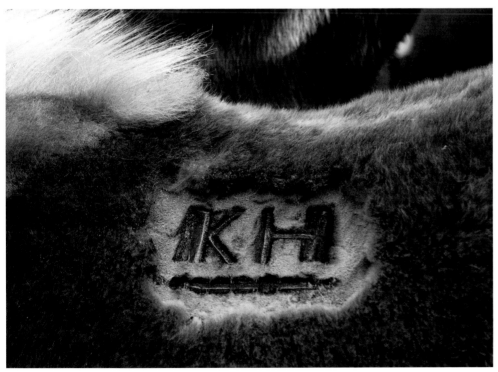

All ponies that run on the Forest must bear the owner's registered brand. Hot branding is much the cheapest and most satisfactory way of identifying a pony. The foal is held against the edge of the pound by three or four men while its fur – either around the saddle or the shoulder – is clipped out with special scissors and the branding iron applied by the Agister or an experienced commoner. Despite the smell of burning hide and smoke, the job is done so quickly that the foal doesn't realise what has happened.

Drift days can be long days. Whole families participate and the children run around learning the skills. Children are integrated into the commoning community at an early age and many take part in the drifts as soon as they can ride. Some start their own herds at a very early age. Honor, Alex and Kerry Humble's baby was given her first pony when she was just four days old and immediately applied for her own brand – 'HH'.

Beaulieu Road Sales Yard

The Beaulieu Road Sales organised by the New Forest Livestock Society are held once a month during the drift season, with an additional sale in April or May for late foals. Ponies selected for sale by their owners only have a short distance to travel to the Beaulieu Road Sales Yard which is in the heart of the Forest. The sales have become well-established as the place to buy either broken ponies or unbroken feral stock and they attract buyers from far and wide. Entries for sale have to be made well in advance of the sale day in order for the details of the stock to make it into the catalogue. The sales days are very busy with horse boxes and trailers from all over the Forest bringing stock for the obligitory before-sale inspection by the vet and by the stewards of the New Forest Livestock Society. Any animal that is unwell, not fit to travel or immature may be rejected from the sale on inspection.

Once the ponies are declared healthy, they are given their sale number, sorted by size and moved to holding pens where they can be viewed by potential buyers. All the pens in the yard are made of Forest timber with gravel floors and are situated on the open Forest, ideal for holding semi-feral stock. Beaulieu Road is acknowledged as being one of the safest and most efficient sales yards in the country and its natural landscaping means it blends well with the surrounding countryside.

The auction prices are set in guineas. New Forest ponies are much in demand. Their hardiness and their temperament make them ideal riding ponies and this means there is always considerable interest in the sales and stiff competition for good stock. The pre-sale Foal Show has done much to improve the quality and saleability of the stock. All fully-registered New Forest foals are eligible for entry and the show's prize winners go on to fetch top prices at auction.

The sales are vital for the commoners and although some sell their stock privately, most sales of ponies go through Beaulieu Road. The sales are timed to ensure that foals can be weaned and sold immediately, as most commoners do not have the resources to keep their surplus stock. Older mares, stallions, geldings, non-registered ponies, Shetlands and donkeys are also sold at Beaulieu Road.

The Shows

Many commoners like to show their animals. They have a great sense of occasion and enjoy the social side of shows. The New Forest Show, the largest of the year, takes place in New Park, Brockenhurst and is three glorious days of rural and agricultural tradition.

The first New Forest Show, a one-day event, was held in 1921. In 1978 the show grew to two-days and it subsequently became a three-day show in 1989. Held annually during the last week of July, the show attracts 100,000 visitors. It has an excellent reputation locally and nationally and is rated amongst the top five agricultural and equestrian shows in the UK.

There are many other shows held in New Park during the year. The first usually is the Young Farmers' Show, but probably the most important to the commoners is the New Forest Pony Breeding and Cattle Society Show, known as The Breed Show. This three-day show at the end of August celebrated its centenary in 2006. New Forest Pony owners travel from all over Europe to show their ponies – both Forest and stud bred.

The New Forest Point-to-Point

When the drift season is over, the highlight in the New Forest commoners' year is the Boxing Day Point-to-Point. It is the only true remaining point-to-point in the country without a set course and very little has changed since the first race in 1912. It is a hard race with seven or eight different classes and the training is rigorous.

On Christmas Day competitors find out where they are to meet, but are given no indication of the start or the finish. Each year the start and finish; which could be anywhere on the Forest, are selected by a knowledgeable commoner. On Boxing Day the riders are led deep into the Forest to the start. The finishing point of the race is then revealed.

The vet measures and checks the horses and ponies before the race starts. Everyone is aware of the hazards and the air is full of nervous tension. Most people navigate the race in a group, but some take a chance and go out on their own and, in the words of one young commoner 'what happens happens'.

The main course is three miles long, a little shorter for the juniors and veterans, and is designed to test the riders' skills and the Forest knowledge of both horse and rider. Bogs, thick woodland, rough heath land, slippery underpasses and many other hazards form part of every course and the finishes are often nail-bitingly close.

When it's over, all the weeks of exhausting evening training have been well worth it to the riders who had a thrilling and successful race. For those whose horse went lame on the day, or who fell off in a bog, there will always be next year.

Whatever the weather, the point-to-point never fails to draw a large crowd.

"Boxing Day is more important than Christmas Day in our family," says Lucinda Ingram whose family had a spectacular year in 2004 when she won the Ladies Race, brother Alan won the Colt Hunters and Brian, their father, won the Veterans.

The Verderers

There are ten Verderers, five who are appointed and five who are elected. Their primary objective is to regulate and protect the commoners' interests and to preserve the natural beauty and traditional character of the Forest. By law, they are not permitted to profit from their office.

In order to qualify to be a Verderer a candidate must occupy, but not necessarily own, one acre of land to which rights of pasture over the New Forest are attached.

The Crown appoints the Official Verderer. The Department for Environment, Food and Rural Affairs, the Forestry Commission, the Countryside Agency and the Planning Authority are responsible for the other four appointed Verderers. They each serve for varying amounts of time. The five elected Verderers serve for a period of six years. They are elected by the commoners for their immense knowledge and unequivocal commitment to the New Forest. Between them they possess an extraordinary variety of skills and expertise. This is the great strength of the Court.

As the demands on the Forest have increased over the years, so too have the demands on the Verderers. In addition to an in-depth knowledge of the Forest, Forest law and animal husbandry, they now have to know about EU regulations and National Park law.

Anyone can attend the Verderers' Court. Any commoner or any member of the public wishing to make a statement or complaint in public on Forest matters, is permitted to make a 'presentment' to the Court.

The Verderers employ the Agisters.

OPENING WORDS OF COURT
Announced by Jonathan Gerrelli,
Head Agister

"Oyez, Oyez, Oyez!
All manner of persons
who have any presentment
to make or matter or thing to
do at this Court of Verderers,
let them come forward and
they shall be heard.
God save the Queen".

The Agisters

There are five Agisters, one Head Agister and four colleagues. They are on call 24 hours a day, seven days a week. They are all commoners with an intimate knowledge of the Forest. Each Agister must be adept at handling all types of livestock, be an excellent rider and able to work on his own and as part of a team in the rough Forest conditions The Agisters are ambassadors for the Forest and dealing with the public is a large part of their job.

As one commoner said as she watched two Agisters handling a wild colt: "Our Agisters are real men, they didn't get their muscles in the gym, they got them on the Forest!"

Agisters go out in all weathers responding to calls regarding problems with any of the animals. They know all the animals in their area well, often recognising them from a great distance. They know to whom each animal belongs and their general condition. If an animal is ill, in poor condition or a danger to other animals, the Agisters have the right to order it off the forest.

The Agisters collect the 'marking fees', the payment a commoner makes for each animal he or she runs on the Forest. This goes towards paying their salaries.

In the late summer and early autumn the Agisters arrange the drifts (or round ups) of the commoners' ponies.

The Royal Oak, Fritham – reputedly once a haunt of local smugglers – has been known as the 'Parliament of the New Forest'. It is the commoners' pub and the back room is still used for Forest meetings. The landlord, Neil McCulloch, is a working farmer and a practising commoner with stock on the Forest. The pub is an ancient building, being built of thatch and cob, with a good space to leave your horse. The Reverend Peter Murphy, also a commoner, can often be seen behind the bar. The pub is very popular with visitors and has a won a number of awards from CAMRA for its beers.

Forest Roads

The stock has the right of way out on the open Forest. When an animal chooses to cross a road, it still has right of way and it is the responsibility of drivers to respect the animals. The New Forest Trust says "Enjoy the beauty of our Forest. Please drive safely within the speed limit and respect the animals and countryside code. Be tolerant of our animals and allow them to continue their work as 'architects of the forest', which they have done for the past thousand years."

There are animal fatalities on forest roads most weeks. Those that survive being hit by a car, often have to be destroyed by the Agister and the owner informed. This is a very difficult part of the Agister's job. There are many hit-and-run drivers, causing some animals to die a long and lingering death. Surprisingly the largest percentage of accidents involve local drivers who should know better. There is a 40mph maximum speed limit in the Forest but, regrettably, not all drivers respect it.

The consequences of hitting an animal are more complex and far-reaching than most drivers would imagine. In 2004, the superb stallion Obershade Highland Fling was killed by a hit-and-run driver on the Forest at Setley. This is the area where my mares run and they had no stallion for the spring.

One day our Agister Robert Maton telephoned to order one of my mares off the Forest. She had wandered far from her area and was calling to a stallion in the local riding school. This sounds harmless, but she had become so desperate that she was attacking the rides of small children as they left the school. This is unusual, but it could have been very dangerous. A careless driver had killed the stallion and, in doing so, had upset the course of nature.

The story ended well. The resourceful Robert Maton arranged to have the mare covered by the stallion at the riding school with the permission of the owner. Eleven months later she gave birth to a beautiful colt foal. Sadly, Forest problems are rarely that easy to solve.

Tourism on the Forest

Since William I established his 'Nova Foresta' in 1079 there has always been conflict between various Forest 'user groups'.

William used the area for hunting and the 'beasts of the chase' were protected under strict Forest Laws. These Laws conflicted with the way of life of the local people. This conflict was later partly resolved by modifying commoning and other rights. As more areas became enclosed for timber production, the commoners' grazing rights were protected by setting aside two thirds of the Forest to remain as unenclosed open land for commoners to exercise their traditional rights.

Today, greater affluence and more leisure time has resulted in huge numbers of people descending with their cars, caravans, tents, bicycles and games onto the Forest's fragile fabric.

Recreation and tourism are of great economic importance to the Forest but the increased tourist population has led to erosion of the land and disturbance of the wildlife by walkers, dogs, cyclists and riders. People feed the ponies and donkeys which encourages them to come to the roadside where they are in danger of being killed. So a very strong message is given out: 'Don't feed the animals under any circumstances.'

The Government's designation of the New Forest as a National Park, has brought mixed reactions within the local community. Special status and the highest levels of conservation and management have been conferred on this unique landscape. However there are anxieties that National Park status may bring with it a huge influx of tourists which will create considerable strain on the very fragile ecology of the Forest.

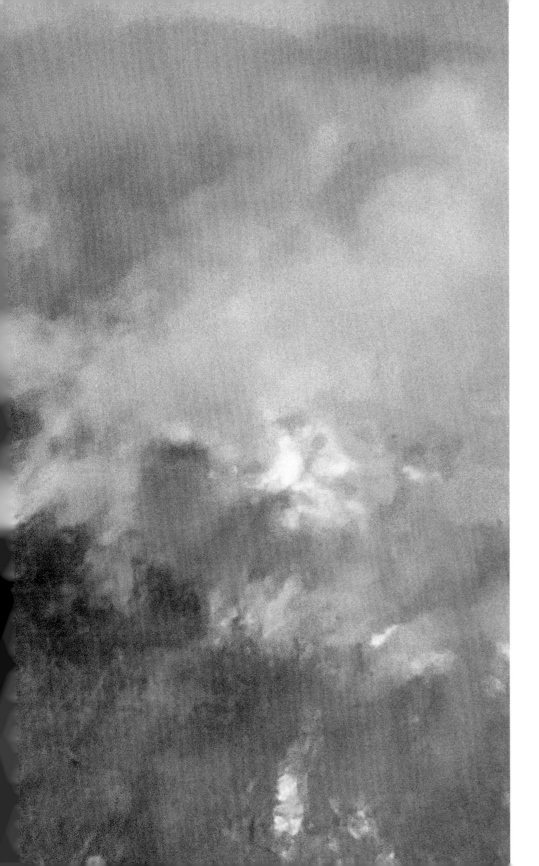

The Ecology of the New Forest

The sight of flaming heathlands can be alarming, but the fires are strictly managed and the wildlife benefits immensely. The burning takes place between 1st November and 31st March, which is determined by the 'National Heather and Grass Burning Code'. It is done when the ground is still wet in order to avoid harming roots or animals below the soil surface.

The Forestry Commission are obliged to keep areas of grazing clear for commoners' animals. Controlled burning is an effective method of removing foliage and maintaining the low nutrient levels required of heathland habitat. The burning of specified areas each year creates a mosaic of diverse vegetation structure and habitats for many of the species for which the New Forest is well known. Dartford warblers can be found in patchy young gorse amongst the heather, whereas open ground free of dense vegetation is preferred by woodlarks, often to be found at recently burnt sites. The open heath is also an ideal nesting and feeding territory for the nightjar.

Animals have been grazing the New Forest for 1,000 years and this has produced its own peculiar habitat. It has a fragile ecology so it is important not to disturb the ancient ways.

94

Stock on the Forest

The numbers of depastured animals on the Forest varies from year to year. In 2005 there were approximately 4,300 ponies, 2,750 cattle, 100 donkeys and 200 pigs.

The New Forest pony is much more than a tourist attraction. It is essential for the survival of this ancient pastured woodland. The ponies don't just graze, they also browse, eating and enjoying the nutritional gorse, holly, ivy and brambles. They grow thick, bristly moustaches to protect their muzzles. In winter, their thick coats provide them with warmth and the dense bushes provide excellent shelter from wind and driving rain.

The Verderers' Stallion Scheme has improved the stock of ponies on the Forest. The scheme selects the finest stallions – usually around 42 – and restricts the amount of time they stay on the Forest. The stallion inspections take place once a year and generally any mature stallion that is not selected is kept in the owner's fields. The younger colts (stallions) are castrated to be riding ponies. Commoners can also apply for their mares to be graded. They are judged on conformation, movement and type. This ensures that the quality of foals now being born on the Forest has improved and the sale prices have increased.

Some stallions can be difficult to keep in a domestic environment. During the winter months grazing is made available specifically for the Forest run stallions in New Park, Brockenhurst and on the Cadland Estate at Fawley. Approximately 20 Forest stallions are put in one large field together and after a bit of an exciting kick off,

they quickly settle down demonstrating their special temperament.

Some commoners run cattle on the Forest and these have to be freeze branded or ear tagged with their owner's brand. Various types of cattle dwell on the Forest, including Belted Galloways, Dexters, Charolais, Herefords, Simmental and Belgian Blue. The most distinctive are the Highland cattle. Cattle can be kept out all year but usually come back at night during the winter when there is not much to eat. Some cattle are just turned out in the summer which they love. When Peter and Angie Craton's cattle go out on the Forest for the summer, they gallop around, rolling in the heather and plunging in the ponds much to the bemusement of the ponies. Their happiness and the Forest grazing seems to add to the quality of their meat: the Craton's beef is particularly sought after in Shaftesbury Market.

Donkeys fetch good prices at the sales but they are vulnerable as they are more likely to be fed by the roadside or stolen.

Pigs are allowed onto the Forest during the autumn pannage season, which lasts for around sixty days. The pigs eat the fallen acorns which can be poisonous to ponies and cattle. Some sows which are in pig (expecting piglets) are allowed on the Crown land after the pannage season, but the owners must first obtain written permission from the Forestry Commission. These pigs are known as Privilege Sows. There is a delicious and very distinctive taste to pork that has fed on Forest acorns.

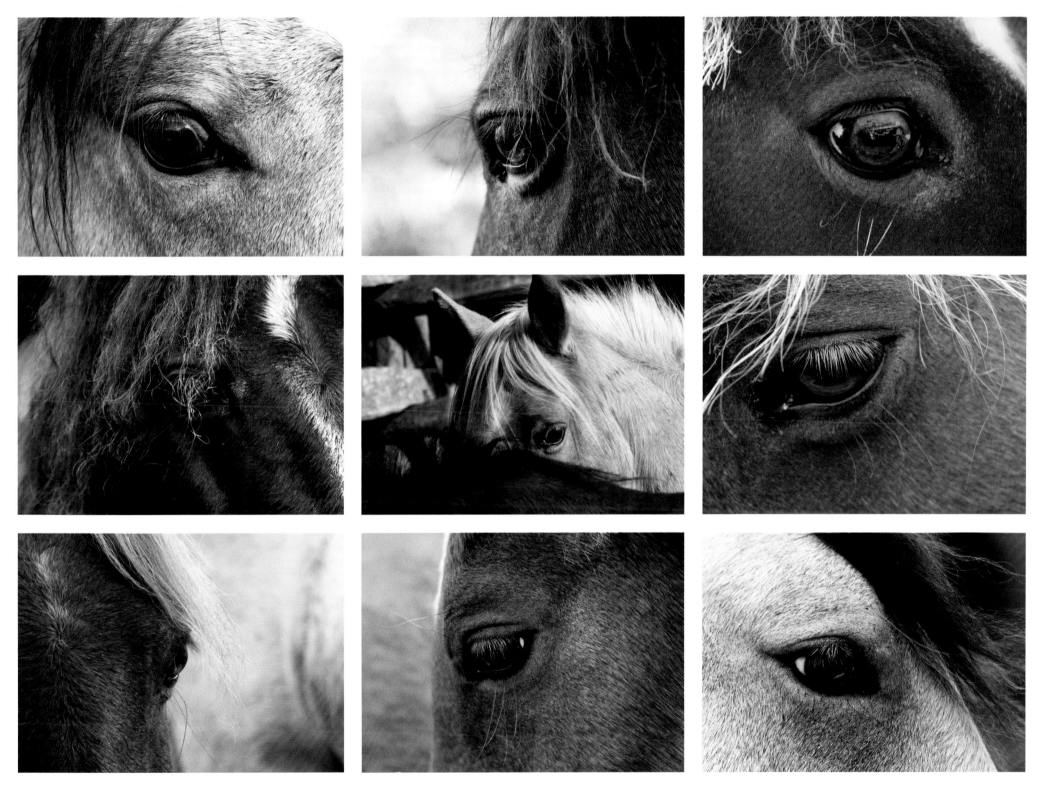

The Rights of Common

The Right of Common of Pasture Pasture is the most important right, permitting the commoner to turn out ponies, cattle, donkeys and mules on to the common grazing. Those who wish to exercise their Right of Pasture do so by application to the Verderers' Clerk who confirms the existence of the right and allocates a brand for the animals. Once they have been branded, the animals may be turned out upon payment of a *marking fee* which helps to finance the cost of employing the five Agisters responsible for supervising the stock on the Forest.

The Right of Common of Mast is the right to turn out pigs in the pannage season. Pannage runs for a minimum of sixty days in the autumn. Pigs are extremely important to the Forest because they eat acorns with no ill effects. Acorns eaten in excess may kill other grazing animals.

The Right of Common of Sheep permits the commoner to turn out sheep on to the Forest. There are very few sheep rights in the Forest and the right is rarely exercised these days.

The Right of Common of Marl The Right of Marl permits the commoner to dig for a special type of clay that is used to improve agricultural land.

The Right of Turbary is the right to cut peat for fuel. Neither The Right of Marl nor The Right of Turbary is currently exercised.

The Right of Common of Fuel Wood (previously known as Estovers) is the right that everybody wants! Under this right, the Forestry Commission is obliged to give the commoner some free fuel wood, measured in cords. There are only about one hundred properties throughout the whole Forest to whom the Forestry Commission grant this right.

In addition to the six registered rights, some properties benefit from additional rights over the adjacent commons, such as the right to dig gravel or cut bracken for animal bedding.

Agisters' Tail Marks indicating their districts

Head Agister
Jonathan Gerrelli

Mike Lovell

Robert Maton

Andrew Napthine

Peter Rix

Commons Animals

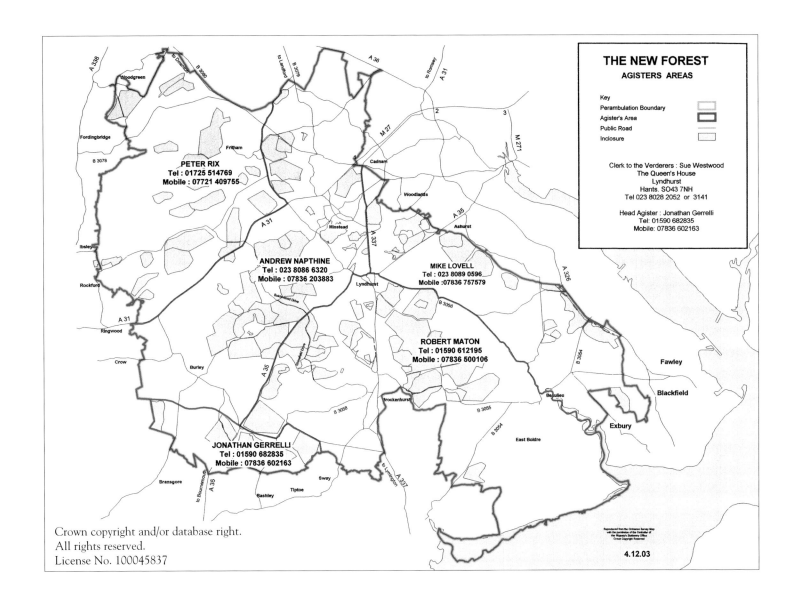

THE NEW FOREST

AGISTERS AREAS

Key
Perambulation Boundary
Agister's Area
Public Road
Inclosure

Clerk to the Verderers : Sue Westwood
The Queen's House
Lyndhurst
Hants. SO43 7NH
Tel 023 8028 2052 or 3141

Head Agister : Jonathan Gerrelli
Tel: 01590 682835
Mobile: 07836 602163

PETER RIX
Tel : 01725 514769
Mobile : 07721 409755

ANDREW NAPTHINE
Tel : 023 8086 6320
Mobile : 07836 203883

MIKE LOVELL
Tel : 023 8089 0596
Mobile :07836 757579

ROBERT MATON
Tel : 01590 612195
Mobile : 07836 500106

JONATHAN GERRELLI
Tel : 01590 682835
Mobile : 07836 602163

4.12.03

Glossary of Commoning Terms

Agister

Agisters are unique to the New Forest. They are employed by the Verderers' Court and are responsible for the day-to-day welfare of the commoners' animals. There are five Agisters each of whom has an area of the Forest under his control. They organise the pony drifts in the autumn.

Blow-up

A term used by commoners to refer to a pony which is being colthunted and suddenly runs out of steam.

Bottoms

Forest name for valleys, where commonable animals spend much of the night feeding on the coarser herbage.

Branding Iron

An iron about 80cms long usually made by a blacksmith. On the end of the iron there is a letter, a number or a combination of the two, selected by the owner and approved by the Verderers, to be his or her brand mark. Ponies are branded on the left side, usually in the saddle area, but sometimes on the shoulder. Cattle are now freeze branded or marked with an ear tag bearing the owner's brand.

Browsing

Besides grazing ponies, cattle and deer also eat vegetation off the ground: holly, gorse, ivy, young saplings and the leaves of mature trees. This is known as browsing and supplements the animals' winter diet.

Browse Line

A very visible line, usually about 2 metres above the ground, where Forest animals have eaten the vegetation. Sometimes the browse line is higher than usual as a result of deer standing on their hind legs to reach higher food.

Clipped Out

The hair of an animal is clipped short at the appropriate spot to receive the imprint of the branding iron. An experienced commoner holds the red hot brand in place briefly and does not harm the animal's flesh.

Clipping Out Scissors

Curved scissors to cut the hair without damaging the skin.

Colt

A commoner's name for a pony of any age or sex.

Colthunting

The art of rounding up individual ponies required for a particular purpose.

Cord Wood

A stack of firewood 4ft x 4ft x 8ft (105cm x 105cm x 210cm) used in the supply of wood for fuel 'rights'.

Drift

An old term for the rounding-up on horseback of considerable numbers of ponies or cattle. The Agisters organise the drifts in the autumn all over the open forest.

Driftway

A track or lane running between enclosures.

Estovers

A Forest 'right', also known as the 'Right of Common of Fuel Wood'. Only about 100 properties in the Forest have this 'right'. The Forestry Commission is obliged to give these commoners a certain number of cords of wood. The allocation comes with the property.

Furze

Gorse. Pronounced "fuzz"

Haunt

When ponies or cattle are turned out to graze on the Forest they normally will settle down and live quite happily within a radius of two or three miles; hence they are said to "haunt" a specific area.

Holms

A clump of holly trees.

Keeper

Employed by the Forestry Commission, they control the deer population and carry out annual culls. They also oversee the general day-to-day activities on the Forest. There are 12 Keepers.

Lane Creeper

Before the Forest was fenced and gridded, animals strayed down roads and lanes well boundary, outside the Forest where the roadside grazing was attractive. They were called "lane creepers".

Marking Fee

The fee (£20) paid by the commoners to the Verderers for each animal turned out on the Forest. The fee is collected by Agisters who ensure each animal is tail marked and branded.

Marl

A Forest right which permits the commoner to dig for a special type of clay that is used to improve agricultural land, or for the building of cottages. Not currently executed.

Mast

A Forest right which entitles the commoner to turn out his pigs during the pannage season.

Open Forest, **Open Waste** or **Crown Land**

The commonable lands of the Forest in Crown ownership.

Pannage

A season of a minimum of 60 days in the autumn when the acorns fall on the ground.

Passage

A path across a bog, or valley mire, such as "Matley Passage" or "Admiral Murray's Passage".

Perambulation

A grid and fence line, erected under the 1964 New Forest Act to enclose common land. This stops the commoners' animals from straying into adjoining villages and towns.

Portable Pound

A portable heavy sectional enclosure used for drifts.

Pound

A timber enclosure (or corral) built at strategic points in the Forest to facilitate the rounding up of commonable animals.

Presentment

A request, complaint or announcement made in public before the Court of Verderers.

Runs

Similar to "haunts". It can be said that a pony "runs" in a specified area of the Forest.

Shades

Ponies and cattle group together in summer in certain spots where wind currents deter flies. Often they stand head to tail and flick their tails across the face of their neighbour. Some shades marked on 1909 Ordnance maps are still in use today.

Shelling

Refers to a pony changing its teeth. Between the age of two and three, the milk teeth give way to adult teeth.

Small Commoner

A practising commoner deriving a small part of his/her living from the Forest.

Sucker

A foal

Sucked Yearling

A yearling which still feeds from its mother.

Tailing

Occasionally used by commoners to catch foals and yearlings the commoner gallops alongside the quarry and grasps the tail to slow it up thereby enabling a halter to be fitted.

Tail Marking

Every commonable animal turned on the Forest has to have its tail cut to an identifiable shape by the Agister to denote that its marking fee has been paid to the Verderers. This mark also designates the area of the Forest where the owner lives.

Turn Out

To turn out is to depasture animals on the Forest i.e. to set them free on the Forest.

Turbary

An old Forest "right" attached to a holding entitling the commoner to cut peat to fuel his/her particular holding. Not currently exercised.

Verderers of the New Forest

A corporate body which oversees commoning on the Forest. It employs five Agisters and holds an open court ten times a year.

Walkers

Commoners assisting at a drift on foot.

New Forest National Park

by Lindsay Cornish, Chief Executive

In March 2005 the New Forest became England's newest National Park, the first to be created for nearly 50 years. As the first Chief Executive of the National Park, I am delighted to write these few words for New Forest Drift, whose publication coincides with the National Park Authority taking on its full role.

The purposes of the New Forest National Park are:

- to conserve and enhance the natural beauty, wildlife and cultural heritage of the Park, and
- to promote understanding and enjoyment of the Park's special qualities.

Sally Fear's evocative photographs capture this moment in the Forest's history. Her pictures bring to life what it is we are trying to conserve and enhance and will help people understand what is special about the National Park.

The 'drifts' carried out in the New Forest are a striking part of its cultural heritage and a key element in the conservation of its distinctive landscape. Ponies are often described as 'the architects of the forest' and it is the annual round-up that ensures the health and marking of the stock.

Many visitors and even some local residents may be unaware of this unusual seasonal activity. Sally's pictures show the drama and the beauty of the drifts and help us all to understand the importance of this special aspect of Forest life.

There are many stunning photographs to be had in the New Forest National Park: misty mornings among the trees, golden autumn afternoons, sunsets over the saltmarshes. Sally's action-shots show the human and animal interaction within this setting, one that is difficult to capture but with eye-catching results.

I am sure that Sally's photographs and this book will help more people to understand and appreciate the special qualities of the New Forest National Park.

Captions

Page 73

Jonathan Gerrelli, Head Agister, opens the Verderers' Court, watched by three other Agisters: (left to right): Andrew Napthine, Robert Maton and Mike Lovell. The fifth Agister, Peter Rix, was on an emergency call out.

The Verderers sit behind in the back row.
(left to right): Patricia Thorne (appointed by DEFRA), Kathy Heron (appointed by HCC), Dionis Macnair (elected), Oliver Crosthwaite Eyre (Official Verderer appointed by the Crown), The Hon Ralph Montagu (appointed by the Forestry Commission), Anthony Pasmore (elected), Anthony Gerrelli (elected), John Adams (elected), Peter Frost (appointed by the Countryside Agency).
The fifth elected Verderer, Jeffrey Kitcher MBE, was unavailable.

In the front row (left to right) is:
Susan Westwood (Clerk to the Verderers), Mike Seddon (Forestry Commission Deputy Surveyor), Will Parke (Forestry Commission Area Land Agent)

Page 74&75

Agister, Robert Maton, on the Holmsley drift, 2005

Page 76

Jonathan Gerrelli, Head Agister, working in hard conditions, 2003

Page 77

The Royal Oak, Fritham – the commoners' pub.

Page 78&79

A foal protects itself behind its mother in the busy holiday traffic, 2005

Page 80

Roly Bessant, on Rocket, takes a mare and foal across the green during the Fritham drift, 2005

Page 81

Mares and foals coming down the road passed the bus stop in Fritham, 2003. They obviously have right of way!

Page 82&83

New Forest mare walking slowly away from the place where a speeding driver hit her friend. The badly injured pony was humanely destroyed by the Agister and pulled to the side of the road. It is likely that the kennels would have collected the body later, 2003

Page 83

New Forest foal that has been startled by a car horn at Beaulieu, 2003

Page 84

Mare and her foal grazing by the water splash in Brockenhurst Village, 2005

Page 84&85

Agister Peter Rix leads his commoners out on a drift at Broomy. They pass by a group of tourists on bicycles, 2003

Page 86

Cattle wandering through Beaulieu Village. Forest residents and tourists yelled abuse at them, being unaware that the cattle have right of way, 2005

Pages 86&87

Cattle, belonging to Millie May, relax in the sunshine at Beaulieu, 2005

Pages 88&89

Child feeds a pony at Beaulieu, 2005. The pony has her ears back, which indicates that she is not feeling friendly.
The message in the Forest is always "Please Do Not Feed the Animals". Feeding the animals puts both the ponies and people at risk.

Page 89

(top): Cyclist shares the road with one of Angie and Peter Craton's cows, 2005
(bottom): Pig scratches itself, after bathing in mud, 2004

Page 90&91

John Stride, who works for the Forestry Commission, concentrates on his controlled gorse burning, 2005

Page 92

Canterton Blackberry (a graded NF mare) with her newborn colt foal, Black Jack Jones, in front of the newly burnt gorse. (Jack is full brother to Appleberry Tango p.68)

Page 93

A foal peers out from burnt gorse where he has been browsing and grazing, 2005

Page 94

(clockwise from top left):
• Ponies grazing amongst the heather on Setley, 2003
• Mike Ralph's sow in the woods with her piglets, 2005
• Dominic May's pigs meet with cattle on Balmer Lawn, 2004
• Pony browsing on gorse, 2003

Page 95

(clockwise from top left):
• Pony searching for food in water at Latchmoor, 2004
• Alan Gilbert's cow cooling off in a ditch of water, 2003
• Steve White and Millie May's cow feeding on crab apples at Hatchett Pond, 2003
• Kevin Chatley's cow grazing on the outskirts of the Beaulieu Estate, 2005

Acknowledgements

The making of this book has spanned seven years during which time I have had help, both emotional and practical, from countless people.

I have relied on the support of many Forest people including the Verderers of the New Forest, in particular Official Verderer, Oliver Crosthwaite Eyre and elected Verderer Anthony Pasmore; the Agisters and their families especially our own Agister Robert Maton; Sue Westwood the Clerk to the Verderers and her assistant Sally Cardwell; the New Forest Museum; the commoners of the New Forest who allowed me to spend so much time amongst them especially Brian Ingram, Chairman of the Commoners Defence Association and Richard Manley, Chairman of the New Forest Trust, Caroline Stride, PeggyTillyer, the older commoners Len Mansbridge and Raymond Stickland, and the friends who cared for my animals when I was taking photographs; Arthur and Margaret Tucker, Catherine Pope and family.

I could not have made this book without the help and advice of numerous colleagues including Philippe Achache the curator of my exhibition *New Forest Drift*, Dave Raven my computer advisor. David Reed and his Photoshop expertise, Christopher Cormack, Philip Jones Griffiths, Patrick Ward and everyone at Fixation camera repairs.

I am indebted to the Mark Davis Injured Riders Fund who when I broke my back in 1998, lent me the money to buy my computer equipment so I could continue with my photography; the medical team (traditional and alternative) who have held my back together - often with a bit of a song and a prayer – throughout the whole project; Dr. Sarah Jarvis, Dr. Neil Fraser, Dr. Gertrud Mander, Miss Jane Bridges, Mr. John Nixon, Vivian Grisogono, St. Margaret's Physiotherapy Centre, Robert Lever, Beryl Tollady.

I want to thank the organisations who funded my exhibition *New Forest Drift*; European Community NF Leader+2000-2006 programme, Exxon Mobil, Peter Barker-Mill Memorial Charity, Hampshire County Council, NF National Park Authority, Verderers of the New Forest, Lord Montagu of Beaulieu for hosting my exhibition. Sarah Boszormenyi for editing my film *New Forest Drift* and Emma Rigglesworth of Forest Friendly Farming for her support and guidance throughout all my projects.

I would like to honour the memory of some of those who are no longer here: my first husband Hugh Eddison, my mother Paddy Fear, commoner Freda Harding whose idea this project was, and octogenarian commoner Ralph Hayward who dismounted from his horse to pick me up when I fell off on a drift and broke my back.

My gratitude to my husband Richard Harris-Jones who brought me to the New Forest, gave me a base at Tile Barn Farm, and has supported my work throughout.

Finally my heartfelt appreciation to my friends, Julian and Clare Calder at Perspective Photo Press and their designer Louise Millar. It has been their encouragement, dedication and sound advice, which has made the book possible.

New Forest Organisations

If you would like to know more about the importance of commoning to the New Forest, you might like to look at some of these websites:

www.verderers.org.uk
www.newforestcomoners.co.uk
www.nfls.org
www.newforestpony.com
www.newforesttrust.org.uk
www.newforestonline.biz/nfa

www.newforestnpa.gov.uk
www.newforestmuseum.org.uk
www.forestfriendlyfarming.org.uk
www.forestry.gov.uk/newforest
www.nfed.co.uk
www.newforestdrift.com